82004290R00057

Made in the USA
Middletown, DE
30 July 2018